claudia mcquillan

PHOTOGRAPHS BY
pete mcarthur

chips and dips

more than
50 terrific recipes

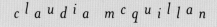

CHRONICLE BOOKS
SAN FRANCISCO

LIBRARY OF CONGRESS CATALOGING-IN-PUBLICATION DATA:
McQuillan, Claudia.
  Chips and dips: more than 50 terrific recipes / by Claudia McQuillan; photographs by Pete McArthur.
    p. cm.
    Includes index.
    ISBN 0-8118-1271-5 (hc)
    1. Dips (Appetizers)   I. Title.
TX740.M36 1997   96-28038
641.8'12—dc20   CIP

PRINTED IN HONG KONG.

DESIGNED BY MARION ENGLISH, ASSISTED BY
        RAMSEY RICKART, SLAUGHTER-HANSON
FOOD STYLING BY KIMBERLY HUSON
PROP STYLING BY CATHERINE HUGHES
KIMBERLY HUSON WOULD LIKE TO ACKNOWLEDGE
ASSOCIATE FOOD STYLIST ALISON ATTENBOROUGH.
CATHERINE HUGHES WOULD LIKE TO ACKNOWLEDGE
FREE HAND, NEW STONE AGE, AND CIVILIZATION FOR PROPPING.

DISTRIBUTED IN CANADA BY RAINCOAST BOOKS
8680 CAMBIE STREET, VANCOUVER BC V6P 6M9

10 9 8 7 6 5 4 3 2 1

CHRONICLE BOOKS
85 SECOND STREET
SAN FRANCISCO CA
9   4   1   0   5

WEB SITE: WWW.CHRONBOOKS.COM

TO NANCY,
my mother, whose
faith, humor, and
inner strength
inspire
all who know her.

SECTION 1

SECTION 2

CONTENTS

SECTION 3

A C K N O W

L E D G E

M E N T S

THIS BOOK WAS NOT A SOLITARY EFFORT. WITHOUT THE SUPPORT, GUIDANCE, AND OCCASIONAL HARASSMENT OF THOSE CLOSEST TO ME, IT MIGHT NEVER HAVE BEEN COMPLETED. WHILE IT WOULD TAKE A SEPARATE BOOK TO THANK EVERYONE I FEEL INDEBTED TO, CERTAIN PEOPLE CANNOT GO UNMENTIONED.

FOREMOST, my heartfelt thanks to Judith Weber, whose patience and strength are beyond my comprehension. In spite of the many roadblocks we've faced over the years, you've never said the words I've expected to hear, and have always stood by me. Words rarely fail me, but I can't express the depth of my appreciation.

Despite my kitchen plumbing failing the first time he came for dinner, and two tiny abandoned kittens I'd adopted running up and down his pant legs, Bill LeBlond pursued me to write a book for Chronicle from the first time we met in Florida. Bill's idea for this book grew into a project that I've thoroughly enjoyed, and I'm looking forward to the next one.

When Leslie Jonath was given my book to edit, I know she had no idea what she was getting into. Despite all my craziness, she never seemed to lose hope that this book would actually come together. Karen Johnson, my copy editor, had amazing fortitude and patience, showing me how to be truly consistent in my choice of words and directions.

As the jingle on the TV sitcom *Friends* says, "I'll be there for you," and my friends certainly have. I would like to thank:

— *Johanne Killeen and George Germon, for being the best friends one can have.*

— *Irma Rodriguez and Rosemary Jimenez, who keep me on an even keel, getting me to laugh at my foibles and see through to the real meaning of things.*

— *Bonnie and Alan Engle and Jason and Gail Asch, who are always there, ready to share the most personal of problems, the best food, wine, and tequila, and an appreciation of the arts.*

— *Nancy and John Arum and Kate Schlesinger, who listened, commented, tasted, and made me Rice Krispie treats and mimosas when all else failed.*

8

— *Nancy Silverton, Mark Peel, Brad Springer, Terry, Claudio, and the gang at Campanile/La Brea Bakery, who fed me great bread, cheese, and fava beans, all the while assuring me (when I was past deadline) that my book couldn't be later than Nancy's.*

— *Nobu, Michael, Maki, and Yoshi, who always found a place for me at Matsuhisa when I needed refueling, inspiration, and a kind word.*

— *Winston Stona, who never fails to turn up at the most crucial times.*

— *The Gonda gang, et al., who helped me move my life in a new direction and into a safe new home.*

— *Neela Paniz, Carolyn Johnson, Zov Karamardian, and the women of LDEI/LA who are an awesome bunch of dames.*

— *Lauren Groveman, a mensch, great cook, fabulous friend, and Ma Bell's favorite customer.*

— *Julia Child, Wolfgang Puck, Graham Kerr, and Maida Heatter, for inspiring me to cook, appreciate the senses, and seek out the finest ingredients.*

— *Jane Matyas, Judy Gethers, and Irv Gronsky, my mentors and cohorts. When my buddies tease me about what I want to be when I grow up, my honest reply is the three of you rolled into one.*

— *John Miller, for being there when life was chaos, and for helping me focus on my desire to write.*

— *My sister Mary, who always thinks the latest thing I've cooked is the best.*

— *Nancy McQuillan, my mother and best friend, whose unshakable faith that I could do anything I set out to do has been occasionally daunting over the years. My great-aunt Rose used to say there should always be one person in your life who thinks you're perfect and loves you unconditionally. I have the great fortune to say that person is my mother, without whose support and understanding I wouldn't be here today.*

9

ENTERTAINING HAS ALWAYS BEEN SECOND NATURE TO ME. FROM TEA PARTIES IN SIXTH GRADE TO TWELVE-COURSE DINNER PARTIES AS AN ADULT, ONE OF MY GREATEST PLEASURES IS TO COOK FOR FRIENDS AND FAMILY. THE INTERESTING PARADOX IS THAT THE MORE ACCOMPLISHED MY CULINARY SKILLS HAVE BECOME, THE LESS TIME I HAVE IN THE KITCHEN.

GONE ARE THE WEEKLY DINNER PARTIES AND WINE TASTINGS MY FRIENDS AND I USED TO GIVE. WE STILL TRY TO GET TOGETHER OFTEN, BUT OUR ENTERTAINING STYLE HAS CERTAINLY CHANGED. WE ALL APPRECIATE FOOD, FROM THE MOST BASIC DISHES TO THE MOST EXOTIC, AND WE REFUSE TO COMPROMISE ON THE QUALITY, YET IT'S THE TIME WE SPEND TOGETHER THAT WE CHERISH MOST.

IT SEEMS ALMOST INEVITABLE THAT DIPS AND CHIPS HAVE BECOME OUR MAINSTAY WHEN WE GET TOGETHER. THE COMBINATIONS ARE ENDLESS, THE PREPARATION TIME FITS INTO OUR SCHEDULES, AND WE NEVER SEEM TO RUN OUT OF NEW IDEAS. ALSO, OUR NUMBERS ALWAYS VARY, AND SINCE RECIPES FOR DIPS AND CHIPS CAN EASILY BE SCALED UP TO FEED THE MASSES OR DOWN TO FEED A FEW, THEY MAKE A PERFECT CHOICE FOR OUR ENTERTAINING NEEDS.

DIPS AND CHIPS ARE A RELATIVELY NEW PHENOMENON IN THE UNITED STATES. PRIOR TO THE INDUSTRIAL REVOLUTION, DIPS AND CHIPS WERE UNKNOWN IN THIS COUNTRY. IN OTHER PARTS OF THE WORLD, SUCH AS THE MEDITERRANEAN AND THE FAR EAST, DIPS AND CHIPS ARE AN INTEGRAL PART OF ETHNIC CUISINES. FOLLOWING WORLD WAR II, DIPS AND CHIPS CAME INTO VOGUE IN AMERICA AND THEIR POPULARITY HAS NEVER WANED.

THROUGHOUT THE WORLD, SNACK SALES ARE GROWING AT RECORD-BREAKING RATES; IN THIS DECADE, SNACKS HAVE BEEN THE FASTEST-GROWING CATEGORY IN MANUFACTURED FOODS. MARKETED AS CONVENIENCE FOODS, DIPS AND CHIPS ARE LEADERS IN THE CATEGORY. WHAT I FIND DISHEARTENING IS THAT, WITH A FEW NOTABLE EXCEPTIONS, MOST OF THE PRODUCTS LACK IMAGINATION AND FLAVOR.

FORTUNATELY, DELICIOUS DIPS AND CHIPS CAN BE PREPARED IN LITTLE TIME AT HOME. THIS BOOK FEATURES RECIPES THAT RANGE FROM THE SIMPLE AND MAINSTREAM TO THE EXOTIC AND COMPLEX. ALL ARE EASY TO FOLLOW, WRITTEN SO THAT EVEN INEXPERIENCED COOKS WILL BE ABLE TO PRODUCE REMARKABLE RESULTS.

MANY OF THE RECIPES HAVE STRONG ETHNIC INFLU- ENCES, REFLECTING THE GLOBAL POPULARITY OF DIPS AND CHIPS, AND I ENCOURAGE YOU TO EXPLORE ETHNIC MARKETS FOR SPECIALTY INGREDIENTS. ASIAN AND INDIAN MARKETS ARE BOTH GOOD SOURCES. MANY HAVE CHIPS—SUCH AS *POPPADUMS* AND SHRIMP CHIPS— THAT ARE PARTIALLY PREPARED AND THAT YOU COMPLETE COOKING JUST BEFORE SERVING.

CREATING THESE RECIPES AND TASTING THEM WITH FRIENDS HAS BEEN A LOT OF FUN, WHICH IS THE UNDERLYING MESSAGE OF *CHIPS AND DIPS*. ENJOY YOURSELF, BE CREATIVE, AND PREPARE FOOD THAT FITS INTO YOUR SCHEDULE. USE THESE RECIPES AS GUIDELINES FOR CREATING YOUR OWN SIGNATURE DIPS AND CHIPS. GUESTS WILL BE WELL FED AND SATISFIED, AND YOU'LL FIND YOU CAN RELAX AND ENTERTAIN AT THE SAME TIME.

TECHNIQUES

By mastering the following techniques you will be well on your way to preparing dips and chips with great results. Roasting garlic and toasting spices and nuts coax out their fullest, most intense flavors. Many people have dietary concerns, and my tips for reducing fat and sodium will help you tailor these recipes to suit your dietary restrictions.

ROASTING GARLIC

Roasting caramelizes the natural sugars in garlic, mellowing its pungent flavor. No special baking equipment, such as a ceramic garlic roaster, is needed for this ethereal taste sensation; simple aluminum foil works perfectly well.

If you have the time, roast the garlic the night before, and place it in the refrigerator. In the morning, the cloves will be popping up from their skins and easily removed.

PREHEAT OVEN TO 400 degrees F. With a sharp knife, slice off the top fourth of a head of garlic. Drizzle the exposed cloves with olive oil; loosely wrap the trimmed head of garlic in aluminum foil, place in the oven, and roast for 30 minutes. Carefully open up the foil, and roast 10 minutes longer. Remove from heat, cool, and remove the cloves from the skins.

ALWAYS store roasted garlic covered in the refrigerator until ready to use.

DEVEINING *and* SEEDING CHILES *and* PEPPERS

When handling chiles and peppers, it's best to wear rubber gloves and work in a well-ventilated area. Be careful not to touch your eyes or other sensitive flesh while you are working. For some people, even the mild oils in bell peppers are an irritant. Anyone who has worked with fiery chiles and not worn protection will attest that it's an experience worth avoiding at all cost.

TO DEVEIN AND SEED chiles and peppers, cut them in half lengthwise and scrape out all the seeds with a spoon or paring knife. Trim away the stem and inside membranes with a sharp knife and discard.

REDUCING FAT *and* SODIUM

Dietary needs can easily be taken into account when preparing most dips and chips.

IN THE MAJORITY of recipes, the use of salt is left to the discretion of the cook. Rather than using salt substitutes, I suggest a squeeze of citrus juice to bring out the flavor of a dip.

IN THE CHIPS SECTION, there are a number of recipes that are baked

rather than fried. Although fat is used in the bagel chips, it could be reduced, or eliminated and replaced by a sprinkling of low-sodium seasoning.

CERTAIN RECIPES in this book, such as the Lobster Thermidor Dip, are sinfully rich, and there's no feasible way to create a low-fat version. However, the majority of recipes are easily adaptable, and many are not particularly high in fat. In fact, many contain no dairy products. Where dairy products are present, reduced and non-fat cream cheese, sour cream, and yogurt can be substituted with excellent results.

THE KEY to creating satisfying foods low in fat and sodium is to use high-quality ingredients. Often, high fat and sodium contents make up for inferior ingredients. Stick to items that are fresh and flavorful, and you are guaranteed excellent results.

4

TOASTING NUTS *and* SPICES

When lightly toasted, nuts and spices acquire a greater depth and complexity of flavor. Toasting releases their natural oils, and removes any "raw" taste.

PLACE the nuts or spices in a small heavy skillet over medium-

low heat. Using a wooden spoon, stir the nuts or spices constantly to keep them from burning. Nuts may take 4 to 5 minutes to toast, and should be a light golden brown. Spices generally only need to toast a minute or two, and should be removed from heat when their aroma becomes very fragrant.

REMOVE FROM HEAT and cool completely.

5

ROASTING CHILES *and* PEPPERS

Roasting chiles and peppers removes the skin and adds a smoky note to their flavor.

TO ROAST CHILES AND PEPPERS, place them directly on the open gas flame of a stovetop burner or directly under broiler. Blacken on all sides, turning occasionally with a pair of tongs. When charred on all sides, remove them from the heat with tongs and cool completely. Rub off charred skin with your fingers, a kitchen towel, or paper towels.

d i p s

(↔)

southwestern ranchero bean dip

Freshly cooked black beans make all the difference in this dip. If you're short on time, canned cooked beans will work, but the results won't be quite as good. Look for the canned chipotle chiles in adobo sauce in a Latin American grocery or a well-stocked supermarket. Serve an assortment of white, yellow, and blue corn Fried Tortilla Chips (page 94) with this dip.

PLACE the beans in a large bowl, add cold water to cover, and let soak for 10 minutes; drain the beans in a colander, rinse under cold water, and repeat the process.

PLACE the beans in a stock pot and add at least 1 quart of cold water; the beans should be covered with 4 to 5 inches of water. Stir in the onion, jalapeño, and garlic, and place the pot over medium heat. Bring the mixture to a boil, reduce heat to a simmer, and cook beans for 2 hours, partially covered, stirring occasionally.

STIR in the 1 teaspoon of salt, and continue to simmer until the beans are very tender, about 1 hour.

WHILE the beans are cooking, preheat oven to 450 degrees F. Carefullly pull back the husks on the corn, leaving the husks attached to the base of the corn, remove the silk, and rub the kernels with olive oil. Pull the husks

½ pound **DRIED BLACK BEANS** *(turtle beans), picked over*

1 quart **COLD WATER**

1 small **YELLOW ONION,** *finely diced*

1 **JALAPEÑO CHILE,** *seeded and minced*

2 **CLOVES GARLIC,** *minced*

1 teaspoon **SEA SALT**

2 ears **SWEET CORN**

1 tablespoon **OLIVE OIL**

½ cup **CANNED CRUSHED TOMATOES,** *with their purée*

2 **CANNED CHIPOTLE CHILES** *in adobo sauce, stemmed, seeded, and minced*

↔

dips   **bean**

¾ cup grated **MONTEREY JACK CHEESE**

¾ cup grated **SHARP CHEDDAR CHEESE**

SEA SALT, *to taste*

2 **GREEN ONIONS**, *green part only, sliced*

back over the kernels, and place on a baking sheet. Roast the ears for 20 minutes, turning after 10 minutes. Remove from the oven, allow to cool, husk, and cut the kernels from the cobs; place the kernels in a small bowl and set aside.

ADD the tomatoes and chipotles to the beans and increase the heat to medium. Simmer for 15 minutes, stirring and mashing the beans until thick and creamy. Reduce the heat to low, add the cheeses, and stir until they are melted. Stir in the reserved corn kernels, taste, and season with salt.

TRANSFER the dip to a chafing dish and garnish with the green onions.

MAKES ③ CUPS

s p i c y

SERVE HOT
TEMP

frijoles refritos dip

A favorite at parties, Mexican-flavored refried bean dip is best served warm or at room temperature. Originally conceived as a way to use up leftover beans, the dip now exists on its own merits. Although this recipe calls for canned beans, revert to the origins of the dip and substitute any leftover beans you have on hand. Try serving Flour Tortilla Chips (page 96) as a change from traditional corn chips with this dip.

DRAIN the beans, reserving the liquid.

IN A LARGE SKILLET, heat the oil over medium heat and sauté the garlic for 1 minute; add the beans, and mash the beans with a fork or potato masher as they heat. When the beans are mashed and heated through, add 3 tablespoons of the reserved bean liquid and the chili powder and cook, stirring constantly, for 3 minutes.

STIR in the cheese, diced chiles, and salt, and reduce heat to low. Continue cooking, stirring often, until the cheese has melted.

TRANSFER the dip to a chafing dish, and serve warm.

MAKES ② CUPS

One 15-ounce can (2 cups) RED KIDNEY BEANS, and their liquid

2 tablespoons SAFFLOWER OIL

1 CLOVE GARLIC, minced

2 teaspoons CHILI POWDER

1 cup grated SHARP CHEDDAR CHEESE (approximately 4 ounces)

2 tablespoons diced canned MILD GREEN CHILES

½ teaspoon SEA SALT

SERVE WARM
TEMP

spicy

dips   bean

campanile's fresh fava bean dip

Every week Nancy Silverton and Mark Peel, chef owners of two Los Angeles culinary meccas, Campanile Restaurant and La Brea Bakery, search the farmers' markets for the freshest and most flavorful seasonal produce. Back in the kitchen, they create dishes that highlight the unique qualities of a particular vegetable or fruit. Fresh fava beans have a very short season in Southern California, but when they're available, those who frequent Campanile know that Nancy and Mark will be serving this dip. Try this dip with Basic Pita Chips (page 91) or Basic Bagel Chips (page 88).

IN A HEAVY POT large enough to hold the beans in a single layer, heat the olive oil over medium heat. Reduce the heat to low, add the beans and salt, and braise for 10 to 15 minutes, until cooked through.

STRAIN the cooked beans, reserving the oil. Place the beans in a food processor fitted with a steel blade and purée; stop the motor and scrape down the sides of workbowl. With the motor running, through the feed tube add as much of the cooking oil as needed to make a smooth dip. Stop the motor, taste, and season with salt and lemon juice.

TRANSFER to a serving bowl and serve immediately.

MAKES (1½) CUPS

3 pounds fresh **FAVA BEANS**,
  shelled and skinned (fresh lima beans are a delicious substitution)
⅓ cup **VIRGIN OLIVE OIL**
½ teaspoon **SEA SALT**, plus
  more to taste
Freshly squeezed **LEMON JUICE**,
  to taste

SERVE ROOM TEMP

dips   **bean**

hummus *bi* tahini

The nutty flavor of this Mediterranean dip comes from the freshly cooked chick-peas (garbanzo beans). Canned chick-peas may be substituted; however, once you've tasted the difference, you'll find the extra effort worthwhile. If you intend to make hummus often, cook a large batch of chick-peas, and freeze in 2-cup portions. The tahini is available in Middle Eastern and natural foods stores. Traditionally served with pita bread, hummus also goes well with Root Vegetable Chips (page 99) and Eggplant Chips (page 97).

1 cup **DRIED CHICK-PEAS**, *picked over (see Note)*

6 cups **WATER**

1 teaspoon **SEA SALT**

¾ cup freshly squeezed **LEMON JUICE**

2 large cloves **GARLIC**

1 cup **TAHINI** (sesame seed paste)

SEA SALT, to taste

1 teaspoon **SESAME SEEDS** (optional)

PLACE the chick-peas in a colander and rinse under cold running water. In a large saucepan, combine the chick-peas with 3 cups of the water and ½ teaspoon of the salt, cover, and bring to a boil over medium-high heat. Boil for 2 minutes, remove saucepan from heat, and let sit for 1 hour, covered.

DRAIN the chick-peas, and return them to the saucepan, along with the remaining water and salt. Bring to a boil over medium-high heat, reduce to a simmer, cover, and cook for 1 hour, or until the beans are tender but not mushy. (As the beans are cooking, occasionally check the water in the saucepan; add more as necessary.)

REMOVE the saucepan from the heat, and drain the chick-peas in a colander; let cool 15 minutes.

(↦)

bean *dips*

IN A FOOD PROCESSOR fitted with a steel blade, combine the chick-peas with ¼ cup of the lemon juice. Process until the beans begin to mash. Turn off the motor and scrape down the sides of the workbowl. Add the remaining lemon juice, garlic, and tahini, and process until smooth. Scrape down the sides of the workbowl, pulse, and taste. Season with salt. If the hummus is thicker than you prefer, turn on the motor and thin by pouring in a few tablespoons of water.

TRANSFER the hummus to a serving bowl and garnish with sesame seeds, if desired. Serve at room temperature, or slightly chilled.

MAKES ③ CUPS

NOTE: To use canned garbanzo beans, substitute one 15-ounce can of beans, rinsed under cold water and drained. Begin the recipe at the point where you purée the garbanzo beans.

thai peanut dip

Traditionally served with satay, Thai-style kabobs, this peanut dip is complex in flavor and texture, but simple to prepare. If Thai chiles are not available, substitute a jalapeño pepper with the seeds removed or 1 teaspoon red pepper flakes. Although I first began making this dip to accompany satay, these days I usually serve it with wonton skin that I've cut into triangles and deep fried.

IN A SMALL SKILLET, heat the peanut oil over medium heat. Add the garlic, sauté for 1 minute, and remove from heat. Place the peanut butter in a medium mixing bowl, and add the sautéed garlic and brown sugar. Whisk in the hot chicken stock, soy sauce, sesame oil, lemon juice, chile, and black pepper. Taste and correct seasonings, adding lemon juice, brown sugar, and chile as desired. Serve at room temperature.

MAKES ② CUPS

1 tablespoon **PEANUT OIL**

1 tablespoon **MINCED GARLIC**

1 cup freshly ground **PEANUT BUTTER**

1 tablespoon **BROWN SUGAR**

1 cup **CHICKEN STOCK**, heated

2 tablespoons **SOY SAUCE**

1 tablespoon **ASIAN SESAME OIL**

Juice of ½ **LEMON**

¼ fresh small **RED THAI CHILE**, seeded and minced

⅛ teaspoon cracked **BLACK PEPPER**

SERVE ROOM TEMP

spicy

mediterranean *lentil dip*

This is a nutritious dip that's healthy and delicious. When tomatoes are in season, try making your own tomato sauce, following the recipe given; however, if it's the middle of winter, don't hesitate to substitute a canned Italian tomato sauce. The finished dip has a lot of body, and I serve it with crisp seasoned Basic Bagel Chips (page 88) and Basic Pita Chips (page 91).

TOMATO SAUCE:

2 pounds **RIPE TOMATOES**, *peeled, seeded, and chopped*

2 **YELLOW ONIONS**, *finely chopped*

4 **BASIL LEAVES**

1 *sprig fresh* **THYME**

1 *sprig fresh* **OREGANO**

1 **BAY LEAF**

1 *tablespoon* **TOMATO PASTE**

½ *cup* **DRY WHITE WINE**

SEA SALT *and freshly ground* **BLACK PEPPER**, *to taste*

TO MAKE THE TOMATO SAUCE, in a heavy saucepan, cook the tomatoes over medium-high heat for 5 minutes, stirring often. Add the onions, herbs, tomato paste, and wine, and cook for 10 to 15 minutes, stirring often, until the mixture begins to thicken. Reduce heat to low, and simmer until the sauce is very thick, approximately 5 to 10 minutes longer. Taste, and season with sea salt and pepper. Remove herb sprigs and bay leaf, and allow to cool. Measure out 1 cup of the sauce for recipe, and refrigerate or freeze the remaining sauce for other uses.

↦

SERVE COLD
TEMP

bean *dips*

TO MAKE THE DIP, bring 4 cups of water to a boil in a medium saucepan. In a dutch oven, heat the olive oil over medium heat; add the onions and cook, covered, just until the onions are translucent, approximately 5 minutes. Add the wine, and cook, uncovered, until the liquid evaporates. Add the lentils, 1 cup of the tomato sauce, salt, pepper, and bay leaves, and stir to combine. Pour in enough boiling water to cover the lentil mixture completely. Bring the mixture to a boil, cover, reduce heat to a simmer, and cook until the lentils are soft, approximately 1 hour. Add more boiling water as needed to keep the lentils covered. When the lentils are soft, the water should have evaporated; if not, cook uncovered to evaporate any remaining liquid, stirring often. Remove from heat, and discard bay leaves.

TRANSFER the lentils to a serving bowl, cover and refrigerate. Serve slightly chilled or at room temperature, garnished with minced parsley.

MAKES ④ CUPS

low ~ fat

3 tablespoons **OLIVE OIL**

2 **YELLOW ONIONS**, *chopped*

1 cup **DRY WHITE WINE**

2 cups dried **LENTILS**, *picked over*

1 teaspoon **SEA SALT**

½ teaspoon freshly ground **BLACK PEPPER**

2 **BAY LEAVES**

1 tablespoon minced **ITALIAN PARSLEY LEAVES**

vegan party dip

This dip is essentially a hummus with a Southwestern twist, prepared with small red beans rather than the traditional chick-peas. Tahini paste is available in Middle Eastern and natural foods stores; look for the chipotle chiles in Latin American groceries or well-stocked supermarkets. Try Basic Pita Chips (page 91), brushed with olive oil rather than butter, to accompany the dip.

SOAK the red beans overnight in cold water. Next day, rinse the beans under cold water. Place them in a large pot and cover with 4 inches of cold water. Over medium heat, bring the mixture to a boil, and reduce heat to a simmer. Cook until the beans are very tender, about 2 hours. Drain the beans and let cool.

IN A FOOD PROCESSOR fitted with a steel blade, combine the lime juice, roasted garlic, and tahini, and process until smooth. Stop motor, scrape down sides of bowl, add the beans, and process until puréed. Stop motor and scrape down the sides of the bowl. With the motor running, slowly pour in the water until the mixture is thinned to a dip consistency. Add the cilantro, chipotles, and salt; pulse until fully incorporated.

TRANSFER to a serving bowl and drizzle with the olive oil. Serve at room temperature.

MAKES ④ CUPS

½ *pound dried small* **RED BEANS**, *picked over*

⅓ *cup freshly squeezed* **LIME JUICE**

6 *cloves* **ROASTED GARLIC** *(see page 13)*

½ *cup* **TAHINI** *(sesame seed paste)*

½ *cup* **WATER**

2 *tablespoons minced* **CILANTRO LEAVES**

2 *canned* **CHIPOTLE CHILES IN ADOBO SAUCE**, *seeded and chopped*

1 *teaspoon* **SEA SALT**

2 *tablespoons* **EXTRA-VIRGIN OLIVE OIL**

SERVE ROOM TEMP

spicy

dips   **bean**

al forno's sweet pea dip

Every time I'm asked to name my current five favorite restaurants, Al Forno is on the list. Tucked away in Providence, Rhode Island, Johanne Killeen and George Germon's Ivy Award–winning restaurant never fails to exceed diners' expectations. This dip of split peas and sweet onions is an example of the clean, balanced taste of their cuisine. Although they serve it with crisply toasted bread from the wood–burning oven, this sweet pea dip is also good with plain Basic Pita Chips (page 91).

WASH THE PEAS and place them in a large saucepan with cold water to cover by 2 inches. Add the garlic cloves and salt and bring to a boil. Reduce the heat to a simmer and cook until the peas are very tender and most of the liquid has boiled away, 30 to 45 minutes. Take special care in the final minutes of cooking, so the peas don't stick to the pan and burn. Add water if necessary.

ALLOW THE PEAS to cool, then add lemon juice and ¼ cup of the olive oil, or more to taste.

TO SERVE, mound the pea purée on a dish, surround it with the chopped onion and drizzle with olive oil.

MAKES (2) CUPS

1 pound dried **SPLIT PEAS**

2 to 4 cloves **GARLIC**, peeled

2 teaspoons **KOSHER SALT**

Juice of 3 **LEMONS**

¼ to ½ cup **VIRGIN OLIVE OIL**

1 large **VIDALIA** or **MAUI ONION**,
  chopped

SERVE ROOM
TEMP

bean

chiles con queso

If you've ever been in L.A., you know that Mexican food is a staple in the diet of most Angelinos. Chiles con queso, *a spicy Mexican fondue, is found among the* antojitos *(appetizers) at most Mexican restaurants and is a favorite of my friends and mine when we're out for margaritas. Unfortunately, many restaurants have resorted to using tasteless processed cheese and canned chiles. Take the time to use real cheeses and fresh chiles (available at Latin American groceries and well-stocked supermarkets), and discover a delicious and quick hot appetizer.* Chiles con queso *is best served with Flour Tortilla Chips (page 96).*

2 tablespoons **UNSALTED BUTTER**

1 white **ONION**, *finely chopped*

2 large **RIPE TOMATOES**, *finely chopped, with their juices*

2 **POBLANO** or **ANAHEIM CHILES**, *roasted (see page 15) and finely chopped*

1 **JALAPEÑO CHILE**, *seeded and minced*

½ teaspoon **SEA SALT**

Pinch **CAYENNE PEPPER**

6 ounces **MONTEREY JACK CHEESE**, *grated*

6 ounces **SHARP CHEDDAR CHEESE**, *grated*

¾ cup **HEAVY CREAM** or **HALF-AND-HALF**

IN A LARGE SKILLET over medium heat, melt the butter; add the onion, and cook until translucent, about 5 minutes, stirring often. Add the tomatoes and their juices, the chiles, salt, and cayenne pepper. Reduce heat to low, and simmer for 15 minutes.

STIR in the grated cheeses, and continue to stir until they begin to melt. Slowly add the cream, and cook 10 minutes longer, stirring often. Taste and correct seasonings with salt and cayenne pepper. Serve hot in a chafing dish.

MAKES APPROXIMATELY ③ CUPS

spicy

SERVE HOT
TEMP

cheese *dips*

winston's jamaican jerked *dip*

This fanciful dip, akin to Welsh rarebit, blends tangy Cheddar cheese with Busha Browne's Pepper Sherry and Spicy Jerk Sauce, for an unusual but distinctly Jamaican flavor. Busha Browne's proprietor, Winston Stona, has become the unofficial Jamaican culinary ambassador to the world and a dear friend of mine. His passion for food and love of his country has created a line of products (available in specialty food stores) that make complex-flavored dips like this simple to prepare at home. Salted Basic Bagel Chips (page 88) or thickly cut Potato Chips (page 101) are good accompaniments.

2 tablespoons **UNSALTED BUTTER**

2 tablespoons **UNBLEACHED FLOUR**

⅓ cup **MILK**

½ pound **SHARP CHEDDAR CHEESE,** finely grated

3 ounces **CREAM CHEESE,** cut into small pieces, at room temperature

4 cloves **ROASTED GARLIC** (see page 14), chopped

3 tablespoons **BUSHA BROWNE'S PEPPER SHERRY**

1 tablespoon **BUSHA BROWNE'S SPICY JERK SAUCE**

IN A LARGE SAUCEPAN, heat the butter over medium heat; whisk in flour and cook, stirring constantly, for 2 minutes. Slowly whisk in milk, and cook, whisking constantly, until the mixture is smooth and thickened, approximately 5 minutes. Add the cheeses and cook, stirring constantly, until the cheeses have melted.

STIR in the garlic, pepper sherry, and jerk sauce, and cook for 2 minutes. Transfer mixture to a chafing dish and serve immediately.

MAKES ② CUPS

spicy

SERVE HOT
TEMP

cheese *dips*

fondue *of three cheeses*

Winter evenings spent with friends in front of the fireplace call for simple hearty fare, like this creamy fondue. Serve it with an assortment of cubed breads and tiny boiled new potatoes, and a sampling of beers from your local microbreweries. This is a simple way to feed guests without spending the evening in the kitchen.

RUB the inside of the fondue pot with the garlic; discard the garlic. Warm fondue pot over medium heat, add wine, and bring to a simmer.

IN A LARGE MIXING BOWL, combine the 3 cheeses. Sprinkle the flour over the cheese, and toss to mix well. When the cheese is dredged with flour, add 1 cup to the fondue pot; stir until completely melted. Continue to add cheese 1 cup at a time until it is all melted. Stir in cayenne, nutmeg, kirsch and heavy cream.

REDUCE HEAT TO LOW, and serve accompanied with assorted cubed breads and small boiled new potatoes.

MAKES (5) CUPS; SERVES (4 TO 6)

1 clove **GARLIC**, *cut in half*

1 ¼ *cups* **DRY WHITE WINE**

¾ *pound* **SWISS CHEESE**, *grated*

½ *pound* **EMMENTHAL CHEESE**, *grated*

½ *pound* **GRUYÈRE CHEESE**, *grated*

1 ½ *tablespoons* **UNBLEACHED FLOUR**

¼ *teaspoon ground* **CAYENNE PEPPER**

Pinch freshly ground **NUTMEG**

2 *tablespoons* **KIRSCH**

½ *cup* **HEAVY CREAM**

SERVE HOT
TEMP

dips   **cheese**

roasted red pepper and chèvre dip

Creamy fresh chèvre (goat cheese) and smoky roasted red bells combined with roasted garlic create a luscious, creamy, full-flavored dip. For a sharper flavor, use green bell peppers instead of red, and fresh oregano rather than thyme. This dip should chill at least one hour before serving. Crudités, Eggplant Chips (page 97), and herbed Basic Bagel Chips (page 88), go well with this dip.

3 **RED BELL PEPPERS**, *roasted (see page 15) and chopped*

8 ounces fresh **CHÈVRE** *(choose one not coated in ash)*

20 cloves **ROASTED GARLIC** *(see page 13)*

2 tablespoons **EXTRA-VIRGIN OLIVE OIL**

⅓ cup firmly packed fresh **BASIL LEAVES**

1 sprig fresh **ROSEMARY**, *stemmed*

1 tablespoon fresh **THYME LEAVES**

¼ teaspoon **HOT PEPPER SAUCE**

Freshly squeezed **LEMON JUICE**, **SEA SALT**, *and freshly ground* **BLACK PEPPER**, *to taste*

IN A FOOD PROCESSOR fitted with a steel blade, combine the roasted bell peppers, chèvre and roasted garlic. Turn on the motor and process until puréed. Turn off motor, and scrape down sides of workbowl. With the motor running, slowly pour in the olive oil. Add the herbs and hot pepper sauce, and continue to process until the herbs are finely minced. Turn off motor, scrape down sides of workbowl, taste, and season with lemon juice, salt, and pepper.

TRANSFER to a serving bowl, cover, and refrigerate at least one hour before serving.

MAKES ② CUPS

SERVE COLD
TEMP

peppercorn ranch dip

This creamy, full-flavored dip will fool your taste buds into thinking that they're gorging on calories and fat. Using freshly squeezed lemon juice and fresh rather than dried herbs makes all the difference. Although crudités might be your first thought as an accompaniment, try blue corn Baked Tortilla Chips (page 93). This dip should chill at least 4 hours before serving.

IN A FOOD PROCESSOR fitted with a steel blade, combine all of the ingredients except the salt. Process until a creamy dip is formed, stopping the machine occasionally to scrape down the sides of the workbowl with a spatula; season to taste with salt.

TRANSFER the dip to a bowl, cover with paltic wrap, and chill for at least 4 hours and up to 2 days before serving.

MAKES APPROXIMATELY ② CUPS

²⁄₃ cup **BUTTERMILK**

1 cup **LOW-FAT COTTAGE CHEESE**

Juice of 1 **LEMON** *(approximately 2 tablespoons)*

1 teaspoon coarsely ground mixed **PEPPERCORNS** *(green, black, white, and red peppercorns)*

1 tablespoon minced fresh **CHIVES**

2 tablespoons chopped fresh **BASIL LEAVES**

1 teaspoon fresh **THYME LEAVES**

SEA SALT*, to taste*

low~fat

SERVE COLD
TEMP

dips   cheese

onion gouda dip

This classic party dip is served inside a scooped-out ball of Gouda cheese. Self-contained, this dip travels well when you need to bring an appetizer to a party. Onion gouda dip should be chilled at least fours hours before serving and actually improves in flavor if made a day in advance. Try serving this dip with Yam Chips (page 102) and Bagel Chips (page 88) made from rye and pumpernickel bagels.

One 10-ounce ball imported **GOUDA CHEESE**

4 tablespoons **UNSALTED BUTTER**

1 small **YELLOW ONION**, *finely chopped*

4 ounces **ROQUEFORT CHEESE**, *crumbled*

4 ounces **SHARP CHEDDAR CHEESE**, *finely grated*

1 teaspoon **WORCESTERSHIRE** *sauce*

3 drops **HOT PEPPER SAUCE**

1 teaspoon **WHOLE-GRAIN MUSTARD**

4 tablespoons **DARK BEER** or **STOUT**

WITH A SHARP PARING KNIFE, cut a lid from the round of Gouda 1 inch from the top, reserving the lid. Carefully hollow out the cheese, leaving a thin wall of cheese on all sides. Finely grate all the Gouda you remove, and set aside.

IN A SMALL SKILLET, heat 2 tablespoons of the butter over medium heat. Add the onion and sauté until golden brown, 7 to 10 minutes, stirring often. Remove onion from skillet and set aside to cool.

IN A FOOD PROCESSOR fitted with a steel blade, combine the grated Gouda, Roquefort, and Cheddar, the remaining butter, the onions, Worcestershire and hot pepper sauce, and mustard; process until smooth. Stop motor, scrape down sides of workbowl, and with the motor running, pour in the beer; process until smooth.

FILL the hollowed-out cheese with the dip; there will be some dip left over. Place lid on ball of cheese and place remaining dip in a bowl; cover both with plastic wrap and refrigerate at least 4 hours, preferably overnight.

TO SERVE, bring the ball of cheese and the additional dip to room temperature. Use the additional dip to refill the ball of cheese as needed.

MAKES APPROXIMATELY ② CUPS

SERVE ROOM
TEMP

golden *caviar* dip

Caviar always impresses guests, and this dip is perfect for a large gathering. It can be made with the roe of white fish, known as golden caviar, or with the bright orange Japanese flying fish roe. Serve with plain water crackers or lightly salted Potato Chips (page 101).

¾ cup **SOUR CREAM**

1 ¼ cups **WHIPPED CREAM CHEESE**, *at room temperature*

2 **SHALLOTS**, *minced*

Juice of 1 **LEMON**

1 tablespoon minced fresh **DILL**, *or more to taste*

A few drops of **HOT PEPPER SAUCE**

7 ounces fresh **GOLDEN CAVIAR** *or* **FLYING FISH ROE**

IN A MEDIUM BOWL, thoroughly mix together the sour cream and cream cheese. Stir in the shallots, lemon juice, dill, and hot pepper sauce. Gently fold in the caviar. Taste, and season with more dill and pepper sauce if desired.

TRANSFER to a serving bowl, cover, and refrigerate until ready to serve.

MAKES (2 ½) CUPS

SERVE COLD
TEMP

bagnacauda

Translated literally, **bagna cauda** *means hot bath. Warmth is generated not only from the chafing dish, but from the amount of heady garlic in this Piedmontese anchovy dip. Serve it as they do in Italy, with warm, crusty bread and raw, roasted, and boiled vegetables.*

4 ounces **ANCHOVY FILLETS** *packed in olive oil, drained*

2 ounces **UNSALTED BUTTER**

¼ cup **OLIVE OIL**

8 large **CLOVES GARLIC**, *halved*

2 tablespoons minced fresh **ITALIAN PARSLEY**

IN A FOOD PROCESSOR, fitted with a steel blade, combine the anchovy fillets, butter, olive oil, and garlic; process 1 minute, scrape down sides of workbowl, and pulse to finish mixing ingredients. Transfer dip to small saucepan, and cook over medium heat for 5 minutes.

TRANSFER to a chafing dish, garnish with parsley, and serve warm.

MAKES APPROXIMATELY (1) CUP

SERVE WARM
TEMP

green *goddess* dip

In our household, we always seemed to be planning the next meal, enjoying a meal, or reminiscing about a meal. My mother often told my sisters and me about a green goddess dressing she used to make before we were born. We asked her why she never made it for us, and she said she could never find the tarragon vinegar called for in her recipe. When I was 12, I discovered Williams-Sonoma, which carried tarragon vinegar. My mother had no choice but to make the fabled green goddess dressing for us, which we thoroughly enjoyed. I've taken the basic elements of my mother's dressing, and turned it into the perfect dip for crudités. This dip is best made a day ahead to allow the complex flavors to meld.

PLACE all of the ingredients in a food processor fitted with a steel blade. Pulse 8 to 12 times to mix, scrape down sides of workbowl, and pulse again 6 to 8 times. Transfer mixture to a serving bowl. Press plastic wrap against the surface of the dip to prevent a skin from forming, and refrigerate. This dip is best served after chilling for 24 hours.

MAKES APPROXIMATELY ② CUPS

1 cup **MAYONNAISE**

2 cups **SOUR CREAM**

¼ cup minced fresh **CHIVES**

2 cloves **GARLIC**, minced

⅓ cup minced fresh **PARSLEY LEAVES**

2 tablespoons **TARRAGON VINEGAR**

1 tablespoon freshly squeezed **LEMON JUICE**

3 **ANCHOVY FILLETS**, minced

½ teaspoon **SEA SALT**

¼ teaspoon finely ground **BLACK PEPPER**

TEMP

dips **seafood**

dilledsmokedsalmondip

I've yet to meet anyone who doesn't succumb to stress during the holidays. With the best of intentions, people plan parties, then find they've run out of time to prepare everything on their menu. I always tell friends, in all sincerity, to call if they need me to bring something. Inevitably, on a day I don't have a spare minute, the host will call and ask me to bring an appetizer. Should you find yourself in such a predicament, this dip is the perfect solution. The ingredients are readily available, the dip takes only minutes to prepare, and the results are always a crowd pleaser. Serve with thin slices of pumpernickel bread or water crackers.

1 pound **WHIPPED CREAM CHEESE**

⅓ cup **WHIPPING CREAM**

10 ounces **SMOKED SALMON**, minced

1 bunch fresh **DILL**, stemmed and minced

1 tablespoon minced fresh **CHIVES**

Juice of ½ **LEMON**

¼ teaspoon **HOT PEPPER SAUCE**

CRACKED BLACK PEPPER, to taste

IN A LARGE MIXING BOWL, combine the cream cheese and cream. With an electric mixer, whip the mixture until light and fluffy. Fold in the smoked salmon, dill, and chives. Season with lemon juice, hot pepper sauce, and black pepper.

MAKES ③ CUPS

SERVE COLD
TEMP

clam*dip*

If you're blessed with access to fresh clams, by all means steam some up and substitute them for the canned clams in this recipe. However, canned clams, when well rinsed, can still make a delicious dip. Simple to prepare, this dip can be made the day before and refrigerated. If you wish to cut calories and fat, nonfat sour cream and light cream cheese can easily be substituted. This dip is best served with salted crisp potato chips, store-bought or homemade (page 101). Be sure to let the dip chill at least one hour before serving.

2 cups chopped **CANNED CLAMS**

1 cup (8 ounces) **CREAM CHEESE,**
at room temperature

1 ½ cups **SOUR CREAM**

½ bunch fresh **PARSLEY,** washed,
stemmed, and leaves minced

2 **SHALLOTS,** minced

3 tablespoons minced fresh **CHIVES**

Juice of 1 **LEMON,** or more to taste

1 teaspoon **WORCESTERSHIRE
SAUCE,** or more to taste

Pinch **CAYENNE PEPPER,** or more
to taste

SEA SALT, to taste

PLACE the chopped clams in a colander, and rinse thoroughly under cold water. Allow the clams to drain in the colander for 10 minutes, pressing them with the back of a large spoon to extract excess water.

WHILE the clams are draining, in a large bowl, blend together the cream cheese and sour cream. Stir in the parsley, shallots, chives, lemon juice, Worcestershire sauce, and cayenne pepper. Fold in the clams, and taste. Add salt, and more lemon juice, Worcestershire sauce, and cayenne if desired.

TRANSFER dip to a serving bowl, cover, and refrigerate at least one hour to allow the flavors to develop.

MAKES APPROXIMATELY ④ CUPS

cioppino *dip*

As a teenager, I often traveled with my family to the San Francisco Bay Area. Restaurants were rated by my parents in terms of which had the best cioppino. This recipe closely resembles the seafood stew that we favored at a Marin County restaurant, except you don't have the fuss of shelling the seafood. Serve with crisp Basic Pita Chips (page 88) or toast points.

IN A LARGE SKILLET, or dutch oven, warm the olive oil over medium heat. Add the garlic, and sauté for 1 minute. Add the wine, tomatoes, oregano, thyme, rosemary, bay leaves, salt, and pepper, and bring to a boil; reduce heat, cover, and simmer for 10 minutes. Remove lid, add the seafood, and cook for 2 to 3 minutes. Remove bay leaves and discard. Stir in the parsley, transfer to a chafing dish, and serve immediately.

MAKES ⑥ CUPS

SERVE HOT
TEMP

½ *cup* **OLIVE OIL**

4 **CLOVES GARLIC**, *minced*

1 *cup dry* **WHITE WINE**

2 *cups diced* **ROMA TOMATOES**

1 *teaspoon minced fresh* **OREGANO**

1 *teaspoon minced fresh* **THYME** *leaves*

1 *teaspoon minced fresh* **ROSEMARY**

2 **BAY LEAVES**

1 *teaspoon* **SEA SALT**

½ *teaspoon freshly ground* **BLACK PEPPER**

1 *pound* **MEDIUM SHRIMP** (*20 to 24 count*), *peeled, deveined, and coarsely chopped*

¾ *pound fresh* **BAY SCALLOPS**, *muscles removed*

¾ *pound fresh* **CRABMEAT**, *picked over for cartilage*

½ *cup finely chopped fresh* **ITALIAN PARSLEY** *leaves*

lobster *thermidor dip*

From the time I was a small child, the family joke was that if I was in a foul temper, the only cure was lobster thermidor. I've never lost my love for it, but these days I prefer to serve it as a hot dip rather than an entrée. It's wonderful cocktail fare for special celebrations, or the perfect indulgence when you feel the need for something rich and sinful. Serve it with toast points.

PREHEAT the broiler.

IN A NONREACTIVE SKILLET, melt the butter over medium heat; add the minced shallot and sauté for 1 minute. Whisk in the flour, then add the sherry, white wine, and chicken stock. Cook for 4 minutes, stirring constantly. Stir in the lobster meat, ⅓ cup of the Parmigiano-Reggiano, parsley, cream, and mustard. Cook for 2 minutes, stirring often. Taste, and season with salt and white pepper.

POUR the lobster mixture into a shallow baking dish. Sprinkle the remaining Parmigiano-Reggiano over the dip, and broil for 1 minute, or until the cheese is lightly browned. Transfer the dip to a chafing dish. Garnish with sliced black olives.

MAKES APPROXIMATELY ④ CUPS

4 tablespoons **UNSALTED BUTTER**

1 **SHALLOT**, *minced*

2 tablespoons **FLOUR**

2 tablespoons **DRY SHERRY**

2 tablespoons *dry* **WHITE WINE**

1 cup **CHICKEN STOCK**

2 cups cooked fresh **LOBSTER**
meat, cut into ½-inch pieces, and picked over for shells and cartilage

⅔ cup grated **PARMIGIANO-REGGIANO CHEESE**

2 tablespoons fresh **PARSLEY**
leaves, minced

1 cup **HEAVY CREAM**

1 teaspoon **DIJON MUSTARD**

SEA SALT *and* **WHITE PEPPER**, *to taste*

2 tablespoons sliced **BLACK OLIVES**,
for garnish

SERVE HOT
TEMP

dips **seafood**

roasted *corn salsa*

Roasting the corn brings out a sweet and smoky flavor while retaining the kernels' natural crunch. Serve with Chunky Guacamole (page 56), Southwestern Ranchero Bean Dip (page 19), and blue corn Fried Tortilla Chips (page 93) for a taste of the Southwest.

2 ears **SWEET CORN**, *ends trimmed*

3 tablespoons **OLIVE OIL**

2 **ROMA TOMATOES**, *seeded and cut into ¼-inch dice*

¼ cup finely diced **RED BELL PEPPER**

¼ cup finely diced **GREEN BELL PEPPER**

¼ cup finely diced **RED ONION**

1 tablespoon freshly squeezed **LIME JUICE**

3 **BASIL LEAVES**, *julienned*

1 small **SERRANO CHILE**, *seeded and minced*

¼ teaspoon **SEA SALT**

¼ teaspoon ground **WHITE PEPPER**

PREHEAT oven to 450 degrees F.

PULL BACK HUSKS, remove corn silk, and rub 1½ teaspoons of olive oil over each cob of corn; smooth husks back over corn kernels. Place corn on baking sheets and roast for 15 minutes, turning corn over after 8 minutes. Remove from oven, cool, husk, and cut kernels from cobs.

PLACE the kernels in a mixing bowl and add remaining ingredients. Taste and correct seasoning, adding salt, pepper, or lime juice, as desired. Transfer salsa to a serving bowl and serve immediately.

MAKES ② CUPS

l o w ~ f a t

SERVE ROOM TEMP

veggie *dips*

chunky guacamole

Some purists feel the only ingredients in guacamole should be perfectly ripe avocados and a pinch of salt. Others add mayonnaise or sour cream, which I think diminishes the flavor of the avocado. Someone tasted my version at a party, and said the only missing ingredient was a splash of **tequila añejo** (golden, aged tequila). I took the advice, and after tasting the difference, I agree. Guacamole cannot be prepared more than an hour before serving, since the avocado turns from green to gray-brown. Serve guacamole with a variety of corn and flour Tortilla Chips (pages 92, 93, and 96) and sticks of fresh jicama.

4 large ripe **HAAS AVOCADOS**

¼ **YELLOW ONION**, cut into ¼-inch dice

1 clove **GARLIC**, minced

Juice of 1 **LIME**

2 **GREEN ONIONS** (green part only), sliced into thin rounds

3 **ROMA TOMATOES**, seeded and cut into ¼-inch dice

2 teaspoons coarsely chopped fresh **CILANTRO LEAVES**

1 tablespoon **TEQUILA AÑEJO**

SEA SALT and **HOT PEPPER SAUCE**, to taste

CUT each avocado in half, peel, and pit, reserving 2 pits. Place the avocado flesh in a mixing bowl, and mash with a fork or a potato masher until chunky. Add the onion, garlic, lime juice, green onion, tomato, cilantro, and tequila; stir gently to mix. Season to taste with salt and hot pepper sauce.

TRANSFER the guacamole to a serving bowl and bury the two reserved avocado pits in the guacamole (this will help keep the guacamole from turning brown). Cover the bowl with plastic wrap, pressing it against the surface of the guacamole, and refrigerate for 30 minutes before serving.

MAKES ③ CUPS

seven layer **guacamole** variation:

SPREAD one-third of the Chunky Guacamole over the bottom of a shallow bowl; top with an even layer of grated Monterey jack cheese, and a thin layer of sour cream. Cover with half of the remaining guacamole; a layer of diced, seeded ripe tomatoes; an even layer of grated sharp Cheddar cheese; and the remaining guacamole. Sprinkle the top with sliced, ripe black olives and serve immediately.

~ spicy ~

SERVE COLD
TEMP

D
i
P
S

57

dips   veggie

pistou *dip*

France's version of classic Italian pesto makes a delicious warm dip for blanched vegetables and boiled new potatoes. Traditionally, **pistou** is served at room temperature, but as a dip, its complex flavor is more fully developed when heated.

4 cloves **GARLIC**, *minced*

2 *cups firmly packed fresh* **BASIL LEAVES**

1 *cup* **EXTRA-VIRGIN OLIVE OIL**

2 **ROMA TOMATOES**, *peeled, seeded, and cut into* 1/4 *-inch dice*

1 *tablespoon* **LEMON ZEST**

SEA SALT *and ground* **BLACK PEPPER**, *to taste*

1 *cup grated* **PARMIGIANO-REGGIANO CHEESE**

SERVE HOT
TEMP

IN A FOOD PROCESSOR fitted with a steel blade, combine the garlic and basil leaves. Turn on the motor, and process until the basil is finely minced. Stop motor and scrape down the sides of the workbowl. With the motor running, slowly dribble in ½ cup of the olive oil, and process until puréed.

IN A SMALL SKILLET over medium-low heat, warm the remaining olive oil. Whisk in the basil mixture, and stir until heated through. Gently fold in the tomatoes and lemon zest, taste, and season with salt and pepper.

TO SERVE, transfer mixture to a chafing dish and sprinkle the cheese on top. Partially stir in the cheese. Serve warm.

MAKES (2) CUPS

tzatziki

Tangy yogurt, crunchy cucumbers, and a fragrant mixture of fresh mint, dill, and Italian parsley create a refreshing dip for a hot day. Salting the cucumber draws out the excess moisture, which would otherwise make the dip watery. Conventional cucumbers may be substituted, but must be seeded before being diced. Serve tzatziki *with crisp Basic Pita Chips (page 88), or as part of a Mediterranean* mezze *(appetizer) platter.*

1 large hothouse (English) **CUCUMBER**,
   peeled and cut into ¼-inch dice

1 tablespoon **SEA SALT**

1 cup plain **YOGURT**

2 tablespoons **OLIVE OIL**

3 cloves **GARLIC**, minced

1 tablespoon freshly squeezed **LEMON JUICE**

2 tablespoons minced fresh **MINT LEAVES**

2 tablespoons minced fresh **ITALIAN PARSLEY LEAVES**

1 tablespoon minced fresh **DILL**

⅛ teaspoon ground **CAYENNE PEPPER**

PLACE the diced cucumber in a colander, sprinkle with the salt, and set aside for 1 hour. Rinse the cucumber to remove the salt.

TRANSFER the cucumber to a double-thickness of paper towels; gather up the edges of the paper towels and gently press out any remaining moisture.

IN A MEDIUM MIXING BOWL, combine the yogurt, olive oil, garlic, lemon juice, herbs, and cayenne; fold in the cucumber, taste, and correct seasonings with additional salt, cayenne, and lemon juice if necessary. Serve immediately.

MAKES 1½ CUPS

SERVE ROOM TEMP

veggie *dips*

aioli with roasted garlic and thyme

Aioli is a mayonnaise-like dip adored by garlic lovers, and usually shunned by most others. This version, which roasts the garlic until it is sweet and smoky, should convert the staunchest enemy of the stinking rose. Aioli is traditionally served with a variety of crudités. My favorite accompaniments are blanched and chilled **haricots verts** *and steamed baby beets.*

IN A FOOD PROCESSOR fitted with a steel blade, process the roasted garlic cloves and egg yolks until the mixture is puréed; scrape down the sides of the workbowl. Add the lemon juice and mustard, and pulse to mix.

MIX the 2 oils together in a measuring cup. With the motor of the food processor running, slowly add the oils to the workbowl, and continue to process until the aioli has a firm, shiny texture. Scrape down the sides of the workbowl, sprinkle in the thyme leaves and pulse to mix. Season to taste with salt and pepper.

TRANSFER the aioli to a bowl, press plastic wrap against the surface to prevent a skin from forming, and refrigerate until ready to serve.

MAKES APPROXIMATELY ② CUPS

10 cloves roasted **GARLIC**
 (see page 13)

2 extra large **EGG YOLKS** *(see Note, page 77)*

Juice of 1 **LEMON**

1 tablespoon **DIJON MUSTARD**

3/4 cup **PEANUT OIL**

3/4 cup **OLIVE OIL**

1 teaspoon fresh **THYME** *leaves*

SEA SALT *and finely ground* **BLACK PEPPER**, *to taste*

SERVE COLD TEMP

beet, chive, and cucumber dip

Growing up, I thought beets came from a can rather than from the earth. When I tried a freshly cooked beet, I fell in love with its natural sweetness and silky texture. Beets are easy to cook and readily available. Serve with crudités or Root Vegetable Chips (page 99) made from beets and parsnips.

2 pounds medium **BEETS**, stems

    trimmed

¼ cup **OLIVE OIL**

¼ cup **SOUR CREAM**

2 tablespoons **RED WINE**

    VINEGAR

2 cloves **GARLIC**, minced

½ teaspoon **SEA SALT**

¼ teaspoon cracked **BLACK**

    PEPPER

1 tablespoon minced fresh **CHIVES**

1 hothouse (English) **CUCUMBER**,

    peeled and cut into ¼-inch dice

PREHEAT OVEN to 400 degrees F.

WRAP THE BEETS in aluminum foil and bake for 1 hour, or until tender when pierced with a knife. Cool slightly, and peel and quarter each beet.

IN A FOOD PROCESSOR fitted with a steel blade, combine three-fourths of the cooked beets, the olive oil, sour cream, vinegar, garlic, salt, and pepper. Purée until smooth, stopping motor occasionally to scrape down sides of workbowl.

CUT the remaining beets into ¼-inch dice. Transfer the beet purée to a mixing bowl and fold in the diced beets, chives, and diced cucumber. Taste and correct seasonings, adding salt and pepper as desired.

TRANSFER the dip to a serving bowl and serve immediately.

MAKES ③ CUPS

SERVE ROOM
TEMP

veggie dips

tuscan-stylecaponata

Similar to the French ratatouille, this dip's origins are rooted in Sicily, but numerous versions are found throughout Italy. This Tuscan version has caponata's essential elements of eggplant, tomato, onion, olive oil, and red wine vinegar, with its own distinctive characteristics. This dip must chill for two hours before serving. Serve with salted Basic Bagel Chips (page 88), Basic Pita Chips flavored with Parmigiano-Reggiano and fresh thyme (page 91), and baguettes, thinly sliced and toasted.

2 pounds **JAPANESE EGGPLANTS**, cut into 1-inch cubes

2 tablespoons **SEA SALT**

1 cup **EXTRA-VIRGIN OLIVE OIL**

4 stalks **CELERY**, coarsely chopped

1 **RED ONION**, coarsely chopped

1 tablespoon fresh **THYME LEAVES**

2 tablespoons **TOMATO PASTE**

1 tablespoon **SUGAR**

½ cup **RED WINE VINEGAR**

½ cup **WATER**

1 cup pitted **KALAMATA OLIVES**, coarsely chopped

SEA SALT and cracked **BLACK PEPPER**, to taste

P L A C E the eggplant cubes in a bowl, sprinkle with salt and toss to coat. Place a heavy weight on the eggplant cubes and set aside.

H E AT ½ cup of the olive oil in a large skillet over medium heat. Add the celery and red onion and sauté for 20 minutes, stirring often. With a slotted spoon, transfer the cooked vegetables to a bowl.

P L A C E the eggplant cubes in a colander and rinse under cold water to remove the salt. Pat the cubes dry with paper towels. In the same skillet over medium heat, add the remaining ½ cup olive oil. Stir in the eggplant and sauté for 15 minutes. Sprinkle the thyme leaves into the skillet, stir well, and continue to cook for 5 minutes.

↔

IN A SMALL BOWL, combine the tomato paste, sugar, red wine vinegar, and water and stir until the sugar dissolves.

ADD the celery and onion to the eggplant, and stir in the tomato paste mixture. Add the olives and cook over medium-low heat for 15 minutes, stirring often. Season to taste with salt and pepper.

REMOVE from heat and allow to cool to room temperature. Cover and refrigerate for 2 hours. To serve, transfer to a serving bowl, and allow the caponata to come to room temperature.

MAKES ③ CUPS

SERVE ROOM TEMP

babaganoush

Roasted garlic and sun-dried tomatoes update the flavor of this classic Mediterranean smoky eggplant dip. Serve with a roasted pepper dip, tapénade, and pita chips for an alfresco appetizer or afternoon snack. For the full flavor to develop, this dip must chill two hours before serving. Tahini is available in Middle Eastern or natural foods markets.

2 **EGGPLANTS**, *approximately*

1 ½ pounds each

¾ *cup* **TAHINI** (*sesame paste*)

6 *cloves* **ROASTED GARLIC**

(*see page 13*)

½ *cup freshly squeezed* **LEMON JUICE**

2 *tablespoons* **EXTRA-VIRGIN OLIVE OIL**

½ **RED ONION**, *finely chopped*

¼ *cup* **SUN-DRIED TOMATOES**

packed in oil, patted dry with paper towels and cut into ¼-inch dice

½ *cup* **ITALIAN PARSLEY LEAVES**,

chopped

SEA SALT, *to taste*

SERVE COLD
TEMP

PREHEAT oven to 400 degrees F.

LINE A BAKING SHEET with parchment paper or aluminum foil, and oil lightly. Place the eggplants on the baking sheet, and roast for 25 minutes; turn the eggplants over, and continue to roast until the eggplants are very tender when pierced with a fork, about 20 minutes. Remove from oven and allow to cool slightly.

CUT each eggplant in half. Scoop out the flesh, place it in a food processor fitted with a steel blade; and process until smooth. Add the tahini, roasted garlic, lemon juice, and olive oil, and process until puréed.

TRANSFER mixture to a mixing bowl, and stir in the red onion, sun-dried tomatoes, and Italian parsley. Taste and season with salt. Transfer the dip to a serving bowl, cover, and refrigerate for two hours before serving.

MAKES ③ CUPS

veggie *dips*

chunky mediterranean olive dip

This dip contains no dairy, meat, or fish, which makes it an excellent choice for vegans. Choose a mix of Mediterranean olives, both black and green, to bring out the full flavor of the dip. Serve with celery sticks, grilled slices of country bread, or plain Basic Pita Chips (page 88).

½ cup **PINE NUTS**

⅓ cup **BALSAMIC VINEGAR**

¼ cup **OLIVE OIL**

1 ½ cups **MEDITERRANEAN OLIVES**, *pitted and chopped*

1 **RED BELL PEPPER**, *roasted (see page 15) and finely chopped*

1 teaspoon **CAPERS**, *drained and chopped*

2 cloves **GARLIC**, *minced*

Zest of 1 **LEMON**, *minced*

½ teaspoon **RED PEPPER** *flakes*

SEA SALT, *to taste*

Sprigs of fresh **THYME**

IN A SMALL DRY SKILLET over medium heat, toast pine nuts, stirring constantly until they are golden brown; remove from heat, coarsely chop, and set aside to cool.

IN A SMALL SAUCEPAN, bring the vinegar to a boil over medium heat, and reduce by half. Transfer to a small mixing bowl, and whisk in olive oil.

IN A LARGE MIXING BOWL, combine the chopped olives, bell pepper, capers, garlic, lemon zest, and red pepper flakes. Pour in the balsamic vinaigrette, and toss to coat. Taste and season with salt. Cover and let stand at room temperature for one hour to allow flavors to meld.

TO SERVE, stir in the pine nuts and transfer to a shallow serving dish; garnish with sprigs of thyme.

MAKES ④ CUPS

SERVE ROOM TEMP

olivada

When you're craving something savory, try this full-bodied olive dip spread on grilled bread, or mix it with diced fresh mozzarella and tomatoes, and wrap it in a slice of grilled eggplant.

CHECK each olive for errant pits.

IN A FOOD PROCESSOR fitted with a steel blade, or in a blender, combine all ingredients, and process until a fairly smooth paste is formed. Stop motor, scrape down sides of workbowl or blender, and process again briefly.

IF THE OLIVADA is to be served that day, transfer to a serving bowl, cover with plastic wrap, and refrigerate until one hour before serving. Allow olivada to come to room temperature before serving.

TO REFRIGERATE for up to 1 week, place in a nonreactive container, and cover surface with a film of olive oil; cover, and refrigerate.

MAKES ② CUPS

1 pound **GAETA**, **NIÇOISE**, or **KALAMATA OLIVES**, *pitted and drained*

3 tablespoons **EXTRA-VIRGIN OLIVE OIL**

2 tablespoons freshly squeezed **LEMON JUICE**

Zest of 1 **LEMON**

2 cloves roasted **GARLIC** (see page 13)

1 teaspoon fresh **THYME LEAVES**

¼ teaspoon cracked **BLACK PEPPER**

SERVE ROOM TEMP

wild mushroom dip

Cultivated "wild" mushrooms give this hot dip a savory, complex flavor. Cremini (also known as Italian brown field mushrooms) and shiitake are my combination of choice, since they are packed with flavor, economical, and readily available year round. However, other mushrooms, such as chanterelles or porcini may be substituted. Serve with toast points or lightly seasoned Basic Pita Chips (page 88).

IN A LARGE SKILLET, melt the butter over medium heat. Sauté the mushrooms, onion, shallots, and bell pepper until tender but not browned. Stir in flour, and cook for 3 minutes, stirring constantly; slowly whisk in chicken stock, and continue to cook until mixture is thickened, stirring often, approximately 10 minutes. Stir in wine, reduce heat, and simmer for 20 minutes.

IN A SMALL BOWL, whisk together the egg yolk and cream, and stir into the mushroom mixture. Taste, and season with salt and pepper. Stir in the parsley and chives, and pour into a chafing dish; serve immediately.

MAKES ④ CUPS

6 tablespoons **UNSALTED BUTTER**

1 pound fresh **CREMINI MUSHROOMS**, thinly sliced

½ pound fresh **SHIITAKE MUSHROOMS**, stemmed and cut into ¼-inch dice

1 **YELLOW ONION**, finely diced

2 **SHALLOTS**, minced

1 small **RED BELL PEPPER**, cored, seeded, and finely diced

¾ cup **UNBLEACHED FLOUR**

2 cups **CHICKEN STOCK**, heated

¼ cup dry **WHITE WINE**

1 **EGG YOLK** (see Note, page 77)

½ cup **WHIPPING CREAM**

SEA SALT and freshly ground **BLACK PEPPER**, to taste

¼ cup minced fresh **ITALIAN PARSLEY** leaves

1 tablespoon minced fresh **CHIVES**

SERVE HOT
TEMP

∂ips   **veggie**

curried sambal

Sambals *are Southeast Asian condiments. In some countries they are used much like a salsa; in others,* **sambals** *accompany curries, and cool down or heat up a dish. This salsa-like* **sambal** *has a spicy curry seasoning. Serve it with skewers of grilled chicken, tortilla chips, or Plantain Chips (page 104). Chill one hour before serving.*

2 tablespoons **OLIVE OIL**

1 small **RED ONION**, *cut into* ¼ - inch *dice*

1 clove **GARLIC**, *minced*

1 teaspoon minced **FRESH GINGER**

1 teaspoon **MADRAS CURRY POWDER**

1 ripe **PAPAYA**, *seeded, peeled, and cut into* ¼-*inch dice*

½ **RED BELL PEPPER**, *cored, seeded, and cut into* ¼-*inch dice*

1 tablespoon minced fresh **CHIVES**

1 tablespoon finely chopped fresh **CILANTRO LEAVES**

1 ½ tablespoons freshly squeezed **LIME JUICE**

3 drops **HOT PEPPER SAUCE**

SEA SALT, *to taste*

IN A LARGE SKILLET, heat the olive oil over medium heat. Add the onion and garlic and cook for 5 minutes, stirring often, until the onion is translucent. Stir in the ginger and curry powder, and cook for 3 minutes, stirring constantly. Remove from heat.

COMBINE the remaining ingredients in a bowl, add the onion-curry mixture, and toss well to mix; season to taste with salt. Cover and refrigerate for 1 hour.

TRANSFER to a serving bowl and bring to room temperature before serving.

MAKES (1 ½) CUPS

spicy / low ~ fat

SERVE ROOM TEMP

ata african red pepper dip

*Akin to seafood cocktail sauce, this fiery dip is a mixture of red pepper paste and chili sauce. In a pinch, **harissa** (a Tunisian pepper paste, available in Middle Eastern and specialty food stores) and commercial chili sauce may be substituted; however, if you make the chili sauce a day or two before, you'll find this dip easy to prepare. For a milder version of this dip, stir in ½ cup sour cream or mayonnaise before serving. Serve with blanched and chilled asparagus and snow peas.*

CHILI SAUCE:

2 pounds ripe **TOMATOES**, blanched, peeled, and chopped

1 small **YELLOW ONION**, chopped

½ **GREEN BELL PEPPER**, cored, seeded, and finely chopped

½ **RED BELL PEPPER**, cored, seeded, and finely chopped

⅓ cup finely chopped **CELERY**

⅓ cup **CIDER VINEGAR**

1 teaspoon **SEA SALT**

¼ teaspoon ground **CINNAMON**

¼ teaspoon ground **CLOVES**

¼ teaspoon ground **ALLSPICE**

¼ teaspoon freshly grated **NUTMEG**

Pinch **DRY MUSTARD**

⅓ cup granulated **SUGAR**

TO MAKE the chili sauce, in a large saucepan, cook tomatoes over medium-high heat for 20 minutes, stirring often; reduce heat to low, and continue to cook until the tomatoes and their liquid have reduced by half, approximately 10 minutes. Stir in the onion, peppers, celery, vinegar, salt, and spices, increase heat to high, and bring to a boil. Reduce heat so that the mixture is simmering, and cook for 1 hour, stirring often.

STIR in the sugar, and cook until the mixture has thickened, 20 to 30 minutes. Remove from heat, transfer to a bowl, and let cool. Cover, and refrigerate until needed.

↔

TO MAKE the pepper paste, place all ingredients except the paprika in a food processor fitted with a steel blade. Process until the mixture is smooth, stopping motor occasionally to scrape down sides of workbowl.

IN A SMALL DRY SKILLET, heat the paprika over medium heat for 1 minute; stir in spice paste, and cook for 3 minutes, stirring constantly so the mixture does not burn. Remove from heat, transfer to a medium bowl, and cool completely.

TO PREPARE THE DIP, stir the chili sauce into the red pepper paste.

MAKES (2½) CUPS

s p i c y / l o w ~ f a t

SERVE ROOM TEMP

RED PEPPER PASTE:

2 tablespoons **RED WINE**

2 tablespoons minced **YELLOW ONION**

½ teaspoon minced **GARLIC**

½ teaspoon ground **CAYENNE PEPPER**

½ teaspoon **SEA SALT**

⅛ teaspoon ground **GINGER**

Pinch freshly grated **NUTMEG**

Pinch ground **CINNAMON**

Pinch freshly ground **BLACK PEPPER**

Pinch ground **CARDAMOM**

Pinch ground **CORIANDER**

Pinch ground **CLOVES**

2 tablespoons **HOT PAPRIKA**

75

spinach*dip*

This dip is essentially a homemade mayonnaise flavored with spinach. In a pinch, susbstitute prepared mayonnaise for the eggs and peanut oil, and reduce the sherry vinegar to 1 or 2 teaspoons. Although I recommend cooking fresh spinach for this recipe, frozen chopped spinach, defrosted, wrung dry, and gently sautéed, may be substituted. Serve with assorted Potato and Root Vegetable Chips (see pages 99, 100, and 101).

2 tablespoons unsalted **BUTTER**

1 bunch **SPINACH**, stemmed, leaves
   thoroughly washed and dried

2 **SHALLOTS**, minced

1 tablespoon **DIJON MUSTARD**

3 large **EGG YOLKS** (see Note)

2 tablespoons **SHERRY VINEGAR**

2 oil-packed **SUN-DRIED TOMATOES**,
   drained and chopped

1 cup **PEANUT OIL**

Freshly squeezed **LEMON JUICE**,
   SEA SALT, and ground
   CAYENNE PEPPER, to taste

IN A LARGE SKILLET, melt the butter over medium heat; sauté the spinach leaves and shallots. Cook, stirring often, until the leaves have wilted and given off their moisture. Transfer the mixture to a fine sieve, and press out any remaining moisture with the back of a wooden spoon.

TRANSFER the mixture to a food processor fitted with a steel blade or to a blender, and process until puréed. Turn off motor and scrape down the sides of the workbowl or blender; add the mustard, egg yolks, vinegar, and sun-dried tomatoes. Process for 15 seconds, then turn off motor and scrape down sides of workbowl or blender.

WITH THE MOTOR RUNNING, slowly dribble in the oil until the mixture thickens. Scrape down sides of workbowl or blender, and process again briefly. Transfer mixture to a mixing bowl; taste, and season with lemon juice, salt, and cayenne.

TRANSFER the dip to a serving bowl, cover with plastic wrap, and refrigerate until ready to serve. This dip is best served the day it is prepared.

MAKES ② CUPS

NOTE: When using raw eggs, salmonella is always a possibility. You may want to use the pasteurized eggs sold at many supermarkets, which claim to be salmonella free.

SERVE COLD

TEMP

athenian *tomato dip*

The better the tomatoes, the richer the flavor of this dip. I make this towards the end of summer, at the height of tomato season. Toursi *peppers, a flavorful type of Mediterranean wax pepper, are available bottled in specialty, Mediterranean, and Middle Eastern markets. Serve this dip with Eggplant Chips (page 97), Tuscan-Flavored Bagel Chips (page 90), or seasoned Basic Pita Chips (page 90).*

PREHEAT broiler.

PLACE the whole tomatoes and onion slices in a single layer on a baking sheet. Broil 10 to 15 minutes, turning often, until the tomatoes are blistered and charred. The onions should be translucent and slightly charred. If they cook more quickly than the tomatoes, remove onions with a spatula to a chopping board, and continue to broil the tomatoes.

REMOVE vegetables from the broiler, and allow to cool for 5 minutes. Coarsely chop the onions, and place them with the tomatoes and roasted garlic in a food processor fitted with a steel blade. Pulse until the mixture is finely chopped, stopping motor occasionally and scraping down the sides of the workbowl.

↔

1 pound **ROMA TOMATOES**, *cored*

2 **YELLOW ONIONS**, *sliced ¼-inch thick*

12 *cloves* **ROASTED GARLIC** (*see page 13*)

1 tablespoon *minced fresh* **OREGANO LEAVES**

1 **TOURSI PEPPER**, *drained and minced*

2 teaspoons **CAPERS**, *drained*

2 tablespoons *aged* **RED WINE VINEGAR**

¼ *cup* **EXTRA-VIRGIN OLIVE OIL**

1 teaspoon **SEA SALT**

½ *teaspoon freshly ground* **BLACK PEPPER**

TRANSFER mixture to a large mixing bowl, and stir in the oregano, *toursi* pepper, capers, and vinegar. Slowly dribble in the olive oil, whisking constantly with a wire whisk. When the oil has been incorporated, season with salt and pepper.

TRANSFER to a serving bowl, cover, and let stand for at least 1 hour before serving to allow flavors to meld. This dip is best served at room temperature.

MAKES ② CUPS

four-onion dip

Sweet onions, leek, shallots, and green onions, carmelized together and spiked with roasted garlic and minced fresh chives, create a dip far more flavorful than any made with a dried soup mix. If you have a stovetop smoker, try smoking the onions over applewood chips for an unusual twist. Serve with salted crisp Potato Chips (page 101).

IN A LARGE SKILLET, heat olive oil over medium heat. Add the onions, leek, shallots, and green onions, and cook, stirring often, for 15 minutes. Add the roasted garlic, cayenne pepper, salt, and vinegar, reduce heat to low, and cook for 10 minutes, stirring occasionally. Remove mixture from heat, transfer to a bowl, and let cool completely.

IN A MIXING BOWL, combine the cooked onions with the sour cream, chives, and parsley. Taste and add more salt and cayenne if desired.

TRANSFER to a serving bowl, cover, and refrigerate until ready to serve.

MAKES ② CUPS

NOTE: If sweet onions are not available substitute yellow onions.

3 tablespoons **OLIVE OIL**

2 **VIDALIA, MAUI,** or **TEXAS**
10/15 onions (see Note), cut into ¼-inch dice

1 **LEEK**, white part only, cut in half lengthwise, and thinly sliced crosswise

6 **SHALLOTS**, minced

1 bunch **GREEN ONIONS**, trimmed and thinly sliced

12 cloves **ROASTED GARLIC** (see page 13), minced

⅛ teaspoon ground **CAYENNE PEPPER**

½ teaspoon **SEA SALT**

2 tablespoons **SHERRY VINEGAR**

1 cup **SOUR CREAM**

1 tablespoon minced fresh **CHIVES**

1 tablespoon minced fresh **PARSLEY LEAVES**

SERVE COLD TEMP

dips   **veggie**

provençal tomato-artichoke dip

Every few years, our garden yields an abundance of delicious ripe tomatoes. One year, there were so many that I came up with a new recipe every day. This dip was created from that bumper crop, and combines my favorite flavors from Provence. Frozen artichokes hearts may be substituted for the fresh, but the flavor won't be quite the same. Serve this dip with the leaves of the artichokes, and with grilled slices of French baguettes.

FILL a stockpot halfway with water, add salt, and bring to a boil over medium heat. Trim off the artichoke stems, and remove tough outer leaves from the base of the artichokes. With a sharp knife, cut off 1 inch of the top of each artichoke. Trim off the tip of each leaf; discard all the trimmings. Rub all the cut surfaces of the artichoke with lemon. Add the trimmed artichokes, lemon halves, and black peppercorns to the stock pot; reduce heat to a simmer, and cook until the artichokes are tender, 30 to 45 minutes, turning them over with a spoon occasionally. Remove from pot with a slotted spoon to a cutting board, and let cool.

WHILE the artichokes are cooking, in a dutch oven, heat the olive oil over medium heat. Add onions and garlic, and sauté until soft and golden, stirring often. Add the

1 tablespoon **SEA SALT**

10 globe **ARTICHOKES**

2 **LEMONS**, *halved*

1 tablespoon **BLACK PEPPERCORNS**

3 tablespoons **OLIVE OIL**

4 **YELLOW ONIONS**, *chopped*

12 **CLOVES GARLIC**, *thinly sliced*

3 pounds **TOMATOES** *(about 12),*
   coarsely chopped

2 tablespoons **TOMATO PASTE**

2 tablespoons fresh **THYME LEAVES**

SEA SALT *and cracked* **BLACK**
   PEPPER, *to taste*

(↦)

tomatoes and cook for 15 minutes, until the tomatoes begin to break down. Stir in the tomato paste and thyme, and reduce heat to low.

QUARTER the artichokes, cut out the hearts, scrape away and discard the chokes, and reserve the artichoke quarters. Dice the hearts, and add to the tomato mixture. Taste and season with salt and pepper.

TRANSFER mixture to a warmed bowl or chafing dish, and place this on a serving platter. Place the quartered artichokes around the bowl, and use their leaves to scoop up the dip.

MAKES APPROXIMATELY (4) CUPS

l o w ~ f a t

SERVE HOT
TEMP

rouille

French in origin, rouille is a dip whose zesty flavor combines roasted red peppers with garlic and chiles, and is thickened with bread. Choose a fruity olive oil to round out the flavors of this dip. Rouille may also be blended with mayonnaise for a dip that is flavorful but less pungent.

IN A FOOD PROCESSOR fitted with a steel blade, pulse to combine the garlic and chile; add the roasted bell pepper and process until smooth. Add the bread and process until a smooth paste is formed; stop the motor and scrape down the sides of the workbowl. With the motor running, slowly dribble in the olive oil until the dip emulsifies and is slightly fluffy. Taste and season with salt.

TRANSFER to a bowl, cover with plastic wrap, and refrigerate up to 3 days before serving. To serve, bring to room temperature.

MAKES (1) CUP

6 cloves **GARLIC**

1 **RED SERRANO CHILE**, seeded and coarsely chopped

1 **RED BELL PEPPER**, roasted (see page 15) and coarsely chopped

1 ½-inch thick slice **FRENCH BREAD**, soaked in water and squeezed dry

¼ cup **EXTRA-VIRGIN OLIVE OIL**

SEA SALT, to taste

spicy

SERVE ROOM TEMP

c h i p s

basic *bagel chips*

Chips can be made out of any type of bagels, but I prefer to use the plain kind. Two of my favorite dips to serve with bagel chips are Dilled Smoked Salmon Dip (page 48) and Wild Mushroom Dip (page 71). The trick is slicing the bagels very thin. One method is to lay the bagels flat and cut them in half top to bottom rather than horizontally. To slice in a food processor, fit the food processor with a thin slicing disk. Place the bagel half on its side in the feed tube, and, using the plunger for pressure, turn on the motor and slice. If slicing by hand, use a sharp knife, being careful not to cut yourself. You should end up with about 20 chips per bagel if sliced top to bottom, 10 if sliced horizontally.

C
H
i
P
S

6 plain **BAGELS**, *thinly sliced*

4 tablespoons unsalted

BUTTER, *melted, or* **OLIVE**

OIL (*see Note*)

PREHEAT oven to 325 degrees F. Line 2 baking sheets with baking parchment.

BRUSH bagel slices very lightly with butter or oil. Place the slices on baking sheets, and bake for 15 minutes; turn over, and continue to bake until crisp and golden brown. If there are too many chips to fit in a single layer on the two baking sheets, bake the chips in batches.

REMOVE pans from oven and transfer chips with a spatula to a cooling rack; let cool completely, and store in an airtight container.

MAKES 60 TO 120 CHIPS

NOTE: You may omit the butter or oil and toast the chips as is, but they will taste very plain.

tuscan-flavored *bagel chips*

Plain bagel chips, seasoned with rosemary, garlic, Tuscan olive oil, and black pepper, and topped with Parmigiano-Reggiano make a great snack, and are the perfect chip for Pistou Dip (page 58).

6 *plain* **BAGELS**, *thinly sliced*

4 *tablespoons* **TUSCAN**
　　EXTRA-VIRGIN OLIVE OIL

1 *clove* **GARLIC**, *minced*

1 *tablespoon minced fresh*
　　ROSEMARY

¼ *teaspoon* **SEA SALT**

¼ *teaspoon freshly ground*
　　BLACK PEPPER

4 *tablespoons freshly grated*
　　PARMIGIANO-REGGIANO
　　CHEESE

PREHEAT oven to 325 degrees F. Line 2 baking sheets with baking parchment.

PLACE bagel slices in a single layer on the prepared baking sheets. If there are too many slices to fit in a single layer on the two baking sheets, prepare and bake the chips in batches.

IN A SMALL BOWL combine the olive oil, garlic, rosemary, salt, and pepper. Brush the mixture over the tops of the bagel slices, and top with a sprinkling of cheese.

BAKE for 15 to 20 minutes, until the chips are crisp and golden brown, and the cheese has melted. Remove from the oven, let cool slightly, and serve. The chips may also be allowed to cool completely and stored in an airtight container.

MAKES 60 TO 120 CHIPS

basic pita chips

This is one of the simplest of all chips to prepare, and is a great way to use up leftover pita bread. Try them with dips that require a sturdy chip, such as Tuscan-Style Caponata (page 64). Basic Pita Chips are pictured on page 89.

PREHEAT oven to 325 degrees F. Line 2 baking sheets with baking parchment.

SPLIT each pita bread in half crosswise into 2 rounds. Brush the inside of each round with ½ teaspoon melted butter or olive oil, and sprinkle with seasoning. Cut each round into 8 equal wedges, and place, seasoned side up, in a single layer on the prepared baking sheets. If all the wedges will not fit in a single layer on 2 baking sheets, prepare the chips in batches.

BAKE until crisp and golden brown, 10 to 15 minutes. Remove from oven and let cool slightly. Serve warm, or let cool completely and store in an airtight container.

MAKES (64) CHIPS

4 plain **PITA BREADS**

4 tablespoons unsalted **BUTTER**, *melted, or* **OLIVE OIL**

4 tablespoons seasoning of *choice:* grated **PARMIGIANO-REGGIANO CHEESE, SESAME SEEDS, POPPY SEEDS**, *or mixed* **MINCED HERBS.**

lemon-thyme *pita chips*

These chips are lightly flavored with lemon and thyme, and go well with a number of dips. Try thems with Provençal Tomato-Artichoke Dip (page 83), Olivada (page 69), or Peppercorn Ranch Dip (page 41).

4 plain **PITA BREADS**

4 tablespoons unsalted **BUTTER**, melted, or **OLIVE OIL**

1 tablespoon minced **LEMON ZEST**

2 teaspoons freshly squeezed **LEMON JUICE**

1 tablespoon minced fresh **THYME LEAVES**

¼ teaspoon **SEA SALT**

¼ teaspoon freshly ground **BLACK PEPPER**

PREHEAT oven to 325 degrees F. Line 2 baking sheets with baking parchment.

SPLIT each pita bread in half crosswise to make 2 rounds. In a small bowl, combine the remaining ingredients, and brush on the inside of the rounds. Cut each round into 8 equal wedges, and place in a single layer on the prepared baking sheets.

BAKE for 10 to 15 minutes, until crisp and golden brown. Remove from oven, and let cool slightly. Serve warm, or let cool completely and store in an airtight container.

MAKES (64) CHIPS

baked *tortilla chips*

If you love tortilla chips but are trying to reduce the fat in your diet, try these baked tortilla chips. They can be made with blue and white cornmeal tortillas as well as the more traditional yellow cornmeal. Serve with the Vegan Party Dip (page 31), Roasted Corn Salsa (page 54), and Mediterranean Lentil Dip (page 28).

PREHEAT oven to 350 degrees F. Line 2 baking sheets with baking parchment.

STACK tortillas on top of one another. With a sharp knife, cut stack in half, and then in half again; cut each quarter in half, so that you have 48 triangular chips.

SPREAD the chips on the prepared sheets in a single layer. Bake for 10 to 15 minutes, turning once. When the chips are crisp and lightly toasted, remove from oven and let cool slightly. Serve warm. These chips may also be cooled completely and stored in an airtight container.

MAKES (48) CHIPS

6 stone-ground **CORN TORTILLAS**

93

C
H
i
P
S

fried *tortilla chips*

How many times have you gone to a Mexican restaurant and filled up on the delicious, hot-out-of-the-fryer tortilla chips? Store-bought chips never taste quite the same. Yet people often fail to realize how simple it is to make restaurant-style tortilla chips at home. Seven Layer Guacamole (page 56), Frijoles Refritos Dip (page 21), and Chiles con Queso (page 34) are all traditionally served with fried tortilla chips.

24 *white, yellow, or blue*
CORN TORTILLAS

2 *quarts* **SUNFLOWER** *or*
SAFFLOWER OIL

SEA SALT, *to taste*

STACK tortillas into piles of 6; with a sharp knife, cut each stack into 6 to 8 equal wedges, depending on the size chip you desire. Spread the tortilla wedges out on paper towels.

IN AN ELECTRIC FRYER, deep fryer, or a deep, heavy pot, pour in oil to a depth of 4 to 5 inches; the oil should not come more than halfway up the side of the fryer. When the temperature registers between 375 and 400 degrees F on a deep-fat thermometer, add a handful of tortilla wedges. Fry for 1 minute, stirring once or twice. Do not crowd the fryer, and fry the chips only until they're crisp but not browned.

TRANSFER the chips with a slotted spoon to paper towels, and season with salt. Continue frying the tortilla wedges, always checking the temperature of the oil before frying a new batch. Serve warm.

MAKES APPROXIMATELY (12 TO 14) DOZEN CHIPS

tortilla *chips*

flour *tortilla* chips

The traditional accompaniment to Chiles con Queso (page 34), deep-fried flour tortilla chips are lighter and flakier than corn ones. Unfortunately, flour tortilla chips do not store well, but I've never found leftovers to be a problem; these chips disappear as fast as you make them. Try with Roasted Corn Salsa (page 54), Southwestern Ranchero Bean Dip (page 19), and Chunky Guacamole (page 56).

12 **FLOUR TORTILLAS**

2 quarts **SAFFLOWER** *or* **SUNFLOWER OIL**

PREHEAT oven to 200 degrees F.

DIVIDE tortillas into 2 stacks, and cut each stack into 8 wedges. Spread the chips in a single layer on paper towels, and allow to dry for 10 minutes.

IN AN ELECTRIC FRYER, deep fryer, or a deep, heavy pot, pour in oil to a depth of 4 to 5 inches; the oil should not come more than halfway up the side of the fryer. When the temperature registers between 375 and 400 degrees F on a deep-fat thermometer, add a handful of tortilla wedges. Fry the chips in small batches, a single layer at a time; remove chips from deep fryer with a slotted spoon, and drain on paper towels.

TRANSFER to baking sheets, and keep warm in oven until ready to serve. Repeat process, bringing the temperature of the oil back to 375 degrees F between batches.

MAKES (96) CHIPS

eggplant*chips*

While most chips are fried in neutral-flavored oils, such as safflower, sunflower, peanut, or corn oil, these chips benefit from being fried in olive oil. Use the thin Japanese eggplant rather than the common globe eggplant, since it is drier, less bitter, and its shape is better suited to chips. The number of chips the recipe yields will depend on the size of the eggplant and the width you slice the chips; for each person, allow ¼ to ⅓ pound of eggplant. Serve with Baba Ganoush (page 66), Hummus (page 24), or Rouille (page 85).

TRIM the eggplants, and thinly slice into rounds using a sharp knife, a mandoline or "v" slicer, or a food processor fitted with a slicing disk. Lay the slices in a single layer on paper towels, cover with another layer of paper towels, and allow to sit for 10 minutes.

IN AN ELECTRIC fryer, deep fryer, deep, heavy pot, or large heavy skillet, pour in enough oil for a 1-inch depth and heat until a deep-fat thermometer registers 375 degrees F. Fry the eggplant in small batches, turning often with a slotted spoon. When the eggplant is crisp and golden, remove with a slotted spoon to paper towels and drain completely. Between batches, allow the temperature of the oil to come back to 375 degrees F.

SEASON to taste with salt. These chips are best served warm, and do not store well.

SERVES 6 TO 8

2 pounds **JAPANESE EGGPLANTS**

4 to 6 cups **OLIVE OIL,** *depending on size of pan*

SEA SALT, *to taste*

root vegetable chips

Most root vegetables make great fried chips but there are a few guidelines to ensure success. One of the most important tricks is not to mix different vegetables when frying; each cooks at a different rate. Also, do not slice the vegetables too far ahead, or they may oxidize and blacken. If the sliced vegetables develop beads of moisture, place them between layers of paper towels for 5 minutes. Finally, keep in mind the color and flavor combinations. Beets have an assertive flavor, whereas turnips are quite mild. Taro root chips are beautiful, but the flavor is not to everyone's liking. Allow a total weight of $\frac{1}{4}$ to $\frac{1}{3}$ pound of vegetables per person. Try these chips with Beet, Chive, and Cucumber Dip (page 62), Tzatziki (page 60), and Rouille (page 85).

99

PEEL vegetables if necessary, and slice thinly with a sharp knife, mandoline or "v" slicer, or a food processor fitted with a steel blade.

IN AN ELECTRIC FRYER, a deep fryer, or a deep, heavy pot, pour in oil to a depth of 4 to 5 inches; the oil should not come more than halfway up the side of the fryer. Heat the oil until a deep-fat thermometer registers 375 degrees F. Fry each vegetable separately in small batches, turning slices often with a slotted spoon, until crisp and tender. Always allow the temperature of the oil to return to 375 degrees F before adding more vegetables.

TRANSFER the fried chips with a slotted spoon

2 pounds trimmed **ROOT VEGETABLES**, such as carrots, beets, Jerusalem artichokes, rutabagas, sweet potatoes, taro root, turnips, and yucca root

2 quarts **SAFFLOWER** or **SUNFLOWER OIL**

SEA SALT, to taste

CHiPS

↔

c o n t i n u e d

to paper towels and allow to drain thoroughly. Season to taste with salt. Serve warm, or let cool completely and store in an airtight container.

SERVES ⑥

seasoned*chips*variations: YOU may also flavor these chips with a dried seasoning of your choice, such as a garden herb seasoning. To take away any raw taste, toast the seasoning in a heavy skillet over medium-low heat for 2 to 3 minutes, stirring constantly with a wooden spoon. While the chips are draining on the paper towels, sprinkle the seasoning over them. Or place the chips in a brown paper bag, add the seasoning, seal the bag, and shake well to coat the chips evenly.

potato chips

I try not to be a snacker, but homemade potato chips are my downfall. I like them sliced really thin and seasoned with sea salt. Russet potatoes are available year round, and are the most popular potato for chips. When they're in season, I make mixed potato chips with Finnish yellow and Peruvian purple potatoes; since their moisture contents differ, fry each variety separately, then mix the fried chips together and serve. Combinations that rank high on my personal favorite list include potato chips with Clam Dip (page 50), Four-Onion Dip (page 81), and Spinach Dip (page 76). Since no one ever seems to tire of potato chips, be generous in your estimation of quantities. Allow ⅓ to ½ pound of potatoes per person.

S C R U B potatoes, and slice thinly with a sharp knife, a mandoline or "v" slicer, or a food processor fitted with a slicing disk. Place the slices in the bowl of ice water; when all the potatoes are sliced, allow them to soak in the ice water for 1 hour.

IN AN ELECTRIC FRYER, deep fryer, or deep, heavy pot, pour in oil to a depth of 4 to 5 inches; the oil should not come more than halfway up the side of the fryer. Heat the oil until its temperature registers 375 degrees F on a deep-fat thermometer. Drain the potato slices, and pat dry with paper towels. Fry the slices in small batches until golden brown, turning them frequently with a slotted spoon. Transfer the chips to paper towels to drain. Between batches bring oil back up to 375 degrees F.

S E A S O N the chips with salt to taste. Serve warm, or cool completely and store in an airtight container.

4 large **RUSSET POTATOES**

Large bowl of ice **WATER**

2 quarts **PEANUT OIL**

SEA SALT, *to taste*

SERVES ⑥

oven-fried yam chips

When making chips, you don't always have to resort to a deep fryer. These chips, which can be made with yams or sweet potatoes, are brushed with butter, and then baked in the oven to an irresistible crispness. People generally eat more baked than fried chips, since they aren't as filling, so plan accordingly; allow ⅓ to ½ pound of yams per person. Serve these chips with Four-Onion Dip (page 81) or Winston's Jamaican Jerked Dip (page 36).

6 **YAMS**

¾ *cup unsalted* **BUTTER**

SEA SALT, *to taste*

PREHEAT OVEN to 475 degrees F.

IN A HEAVY SAUCEPAN, melt the butter over low heat. Line 3 baking sheets with aluminum foil or baking parchment, and brush lightly with melted butter.

PEEL the yams, and slice thinly into chips with a sharp knife, a mandoline or "v" slicer, or a food processor fitted with a slicing disk.

LAY the slices on the prepared baking sheets in a single layer. Brush with melted butter, turn over, and brush the other side.

BAKE for 15 to 20 minutes, turning once. The chips should be lightly browned and tender. Remove from oven, let cool for 5 minutes, and season to taste with salt. Serve warm.

SERVES 8 TO 10

parsnip*chips*

Parsnips, with their delicate flavor, make wonderful chips. Double frying gives these chips their crisp texture. For each person you're serving, allow ¼ pound of parsnips. Serve with Green Goddess Dip (page 47) or Clam Dip (page 50).

PEEL parsnips, and, with a sharp knife, a slicing disk in a food processor, or a mandoline or "v" slicer, cut crosswise into ⅟₁₆-inch-thick slices.

IN AN ELECTRIC FRYER, a deep fryer, or a deep, heavy pot, pour in oil to a depth of 4 to 5 inches; the oil should not come more than halfway up the side of the fryer. Heat the oil until a deep-fat thermometer registers 325 degrees F. Add the chips a few at a time, and fry for 30 seconds, until the chips are limp. With a slotted spatula, transfer the chips to paper towels, and continue frying the remaining chips.

INCREASE the heat to 375 degrees F, and refry the chips, a few at a time, until crisp and golden brown. Transfer to paper towels, and drain thoroughly.

SPRINKLE the warm chips with salt. Serve warm, or cool completely and seal in an airtight container.

SERVES (8)

2 pounds fresh **PARSNIPS**

2 quarts **PEANUT OIL**

SEA SALT, *to taste*

103

C
H
i
P
S

plantain *chips*

A staple throughout the Caribbean and Central America, ripe plantains are eaten like bananas. When unripe or green, however, plantains have a texture similar to a potato, and need to be cooked before they are palatable. In this recipe, unripe green plantains are transformed into crisp and creamy chips through a process of double frying. Green plantains are becoming readily available in the produce section of most supermarkets and can always be found in Latin American markets. Plantain chips are great alone or served with Curried Sambal (page 72).

4 unripe **GREEN PLANTAINS**

3 cups **SAFFLOWER** *or* **SUNFLOWER OIL**

SEA SALT *and cracked* **BLACK PEPPER**, *to taste*

P E E L each plantain, and cut crosswise into 2-inch long pieces.

I N   A   H E A V Y   S A U C E P A N, heat the oil until it registers 375 degrees F on a deep-fat thermometer; if the oil begins to smoke, lower the temperature slightly. Place a few plantain pieces in the oil and fry for 3 minutes, turning the pieces occasionally with a slotted spoon. Transfer the pieces to a triple thickness of paper towels or a brown paper bag to absorb the excess oil. Repeat the process until all the pieces have been fried.

S T A N D   each piece upright on a chopping board. With the bottom of a clean, heavy skillet, flatten each piece into a round, using slow steady pressure.

c o n t i n u e d

PREHEAT oven to 275 degrees F.

REHEAT the saucepan of oil until a deep-fat thermometer registers 375 degrees F, and fry the smashed rounds, 2 at a time, until golden brown on both sides; remove from the oil with a slotted spoon and drain thoroughly on paper towels. Season to taste with salt and pepper.

AS THE CHIPS are fried and drained, place them on a baking sheet and keep warm in a 200 degree oven until ready to serve. Plantain chips should be served warm; they do not store well.

MAKES (16) CHIPS

LIQUIDS

US	METRIC	UK
2 tbl	30 ml	1 fl oz
¼ cup	60 ml	2 fl oz
⅓ cup	80 ml	3 fl oz
½ cup	125 ml	4 fl oz
⅔ cup	160 ml	5 fl oz
¾ cup	180 ml	6 fl oz
1 cup	250 ml	8 fl oz
1½ cups	375 ml	12 fl oz
2 cups	500 ml	16 fl oz
4 cups [1 qt.]	1 liter	32 fl oz

WEIGHTS

US/UK	METRIC
1 oz	30 g
2 oz	60 g
3 oz	90 g
4 oz (¼ lb)	125 g
5 oz (⅓ lb)	155 g
6 oz	185 g
7 oz	220 g
8 oz (½ lb)	250 g
10 oz	315 g
12 oz (¾ lb)	375 g
14 oz	440 g
16 oz (1 lb)	500 g
1½ lb	750 g
2 lb	1 kg
3 lb	1.5 kg

table of equivalents

THE EXACT EQUIVALENTS

IN THE FOLLOWING TABLES

HAVE BEEN ROUNDED FOR

CONVENIENCE.

LENGTHS

US	METRIC
⅛ in	3 mm
¼ in	6 mm
½ in	12 mm
1 in	2.5 cm
2 in	5 cm
3 in	7.5 cm
4 in	10 cm
5 in	13 cm
6 in	15 cm
7 in	18 cm
8 in	20 cm
9 in	23 cm
10 in	25 cm
11 in	28 cm
12 in/1 ft	30 cm

OVEN TEMPERATURES

FAHRENHEIT	CELSIUS	GAS
250	120	½
275	140	1
300	150	2
325	160	3
350	180	4
375	190	5
400	200	6
425	220	7
450	230	8
475	240	9
500	260	10